AF126345

BOOK ANALYSIS

By Claire Parker

Alias Grace

by Margaret Atwood

MARGARET ATWOOD

CANADIAN NOVELIST, POET AND ESSAYIST

- **Born in Ottawa in 1939.**
- **Notable works:**
  - *The Handmaid's Tale* (1985), novel
  - *The Blind Assassin* (2000), novel
  - *Oryx and Crake* (2003), novel

Margaret Atwood is Canada's most influential contemporary writer. She studied English Literature at the University of Toronto and later at Harvard, and first received public acclaim as a poet in the 1960s with her collections *Double Persephone* (1961) and *The Circle Game* (1966). She has since written over 40 works including novels, short stories and critical essays which have been published around the world, though she is perhaps most famous for her 1985 dystopian novel *The Handmaid's Tale.* Her impressive range of work spans science fiction, myth, life writing, and historical fiction, but is largely united by themes of abuse of power and female experience: "My women suffer because most of the women I speak to seem to have suffered", she has said (Klemesrud, 1982). Atwood's later work also explores the process of writing, and as an English lecturer she delivered a series of lectures in 2000 entitled *Negotiating with the Dead: A Writer on Writing*. She currently lives in Toronto.

ALIAS GRACE

A NOVEL OF HISTORICAL FICTION

- **Genre:** historical novel
- **Reference edition:** Atwood, M. (2017) *Alias Grace*. London: Virago.
- **1st edition:** 1996
- **Themes:** murder, guilt, class conflict, sexuality, dreams, mental illness

Alias Grace is a work of historical fiction based on the vicious double murder of Thomas Kinnear and Nancy Montgomery in 1843 in Ontario, Canada. Soon after the victims' bodies were discovered in their cellar, their two servants were arrested; while James McDermott was hanged, Grace Marks, aged just 16, was jailed for life as an accessory to the crime. The trial hears many contradictory accounts of the events, and with Grace claiming to have no memory whatsoever of what took place, a panel protesting her innocence enlists the help of a doctor to ascertain whether Grace is insane and therefore unaccountable. But the more Dr Simon Jordan hears of Grace's story, the more lost in it, and her, he becomes. *Alias Grace* was Margaret Atwood's first foray into the genre of historical fiction after many years of interest in the much-documented Kinnear-Montgomery murder; her novel won the Canadian Giller Prize and was shortlisted for the Booker Prize.

SUMMARY

Having been sentenced to life imprisonment in 1843, Grace Marks has been an inmate of Kingston Penitentiary for 16 years after being charged with the murder of her employer, Thomas Kinnear, and his housekeeper Nancy Montgomery. At the trial, her supposed accomplice and lover James McDermott claimed Grace convinced him to murder Nancy, of whom she was allegedly madly jealous, in return for sexual favours. Grace's own accounts were highly contradictory; at one point she admitted to being present but uninvolved in the murders, but she subsequently claimed to have no memory of crucial events, and was painted as both an "inhuman female demon" and an "innocent victim of a blackguard" (p. 25) by the press.

A reform committee petitioning for Grace's release from prison decides to employ an American doctor, Dr Simon Jordan, to write a report on Grace's emotional state, hoping a diagnosis of insanity will exonerate her. Simon is interested in the burgeoning field of mental illness, and hopes this project will further his career, enabling him to pioneer his own mental health clinic. Visiting Grace every day in the household where she undertakes unpaid work as part of her punishment, Simon asks her to tell him her story while she attends to sewing and mending quilts.

Grace tells Simon she was born in Ireland to a dysfunctional Protestant family. Her alcoholic father decided the family should emigrate to Canada in the hope of acquiring free land. During a turbulent journey across the Atlantic Ocean, Grace's mother died and was buried at sea, leaving Grace traumatised by the idea of her spirit being trapped. Arriving in Toronto, Grace left her younger siblings and drunken father to work for Mrs Alderman Parkinson as a live-in maid on a meagre income. There she formed a close friendship with her 16-year-old roommate and fellow maid Mary Whitney. Mary was fun-loving and lively with 'democratic' views (telling Grace their social superiors are really no better than them), but she died tragically following a botched abortion after Mrs Alderman Parkinson's son seduced her. The day after Mary's death, Grace fainted after hearing the voice of her dead friend say "Let me in" (p. 207).

Grace left Mrs Alderman Parkinson and was taken on by Mr Thomas Kinnear and his housekeeper Nancy Montgomery. She was also introduced to Jamie Walsh, a young neighbour, and James McDermott, Kinnear's sullen and rebellious stable-boy whose unwanted attention Grace frequently rebuffed. Grace reflects that "of all the people in that house, I was the only one of them left alive in six months' time" (p. 243). Nancy was often hostile to Grace in front of Mr Kinnear, and Grace lost respect for her after learning that Nancy had an illegitimate child and was romantically involved with Mr Kinnear. Amidst an increasingly hostile atmosphere, a peddler called Jeremiah (a frequent visitor to Grace's previous employer) told Grace she was in great danger, suggesting she join him on his travelling 'Mesmerism and Magnetism' show. Grace chose not to, but regretted her decision when Nancy threatened to dismiss her. Nancy had already given James McDermott his notice, and, enraged, he began to talk of revenge.

Grace tells Simon she was unable to convince

James not to kill Nancy, but insists she cannot re-member key details about the day of the murder – though she is adamant she had no part in the acts themselves (Nancy was killed with an axe, and Mr Kinnear shot). Despite himself, Simon has been increasingly drawn into Grace's story without being any closer to drawing out the truth. While Grace threads together her narra-tive, Simon's life begins to unravel: his landlady's husband deserts her, leaving her destitute and no longer able to pay her servant. Simon finds himself running errands around the house while avoiding the advances of both his landlady, Mrs Humphrey, and her daughter Lydia. Instead, he increasingly fantasises about Grace, dreaming one day that she is crouched over him in bed, only to realise he is conscious and making love to Mrs Humphrey. Happy to escape his own situation, Simon visits Grace's original defence lawyer James MacKenzie, who shocks Simon by admitting that, in his opinion, Grace is "guilty as sin" (p. 440). Simon then visits Kinnear's house and Mary Whitney's grave hoping discover the truth, but to no avail: "Nothing has been pro-ved", he says, "but nothing has been disproved, either" (p. 451).

Simon becomes protective, even possessive, of Grace, and is mortified when fellow practitioner Dr DuPont is given permission to hypnotise Grace. Grace walks in on their conversation and is shocked to recognise Dr DuPont as her old friend Jeremiah the peddler. When Du Pont's hypnosis begins (with Simon observing), Grace responds to DuPont's questions in a crude, explicit, unfamiliar voice. Under the trance, she says she urged McDermott to murder Nancy, even strangling Nancy herself. But the voice then says DuPont is speaking not with Grace, but with the spirit of her dead friend Mary Whitney. When Grace comes round, she appears not to have any idea what was said.

One of the committee members says that 200 years ago Grace would have been said to be possessed, while DuPont speaks of a "dédoublement" or "double consciousness" (p. 471). Simon remains baffled, knowing any report detailing the hypnosis would be derided. He resolves to take his intellectual and sexual frustration out on Mrs Humphrey, with whom he has developed an intense, sadistic relationship, but arrives home to find her in tears. Mrs Humphrey suggests the two of them kill her soon-to-return husband. Simon kisses her, seemingly in tacit agreement, but packs his belongings and flees the next morning. The promised report about Grace remains unwritten.

Simon joins the army when the American Civil War breaks out, but a severe head injury forces him home and wipes his memory of the time he spent at Kingston. He is nursed by his mother and a young, plain woman he agrees to marry, but whom he often inadvertently calls 'Grace'. The 'real' Grace is pardoned after 29 years' imprisonment, and moves to New York under a false name. There she is met by her former neighbour Jamie Walsh, whom she agrees to marry. Aged 46, believing she has either fallen pregnant or is developing a tumour, Grace sits on the veranda at Jamie's farm working on a quilt design called the 'Tree of Paradise'. Into the quilt, she weaves material from Mary Whitney's petticoat, her own old prison attire, and a dress which once belonged to Nancy Montgomery. "And so", she says, "we will all be together" (p. 534).

CHARACTER STUDY

GRACE MARKS

Auburn-haired, Irish immigrant Grace Marks – both real historical figure and fictional character – is the central figure in Atwood's novel, though as its title suggests, no one true version of Grace emerges throughout. Instead, Grace's character is full of contradictions, enabling her to simultaneously embody the personas of a cold-hearted murderess and an innocent victim of circumstance. Her prudish demeanour in her first-person narration is deeply at odds with James McDermott's claim she promised him sexual favours and was jealous of Nancy's male attention. Her lack of memory of crucial events belies her stories containing a thousand embellished details, and her ostensibly honest, respectful, almost naïve character contrasts with the kind of woman who would wear the clothes of her murder victim to trial, or who practises rolling the word 'murderess' off her tongue. Young, beautiful, and of a low class, throughout her life

Grace repeatedly finds herself the object and victim of male fantasies of domination (from assault by her defence lawyer to Thomas Kinnear's sexual interest in her). But she is intelligent and a gifted, though unreliable, storyteller; as a result, both Simon Jordan and the reader are drawn almost against their wills into her world, though still unsure whether she is innocent or guilty, possessed or mentally ill. Ultimately, Grace cleverly shifts the balance of power through her intricately embroidered narration, allowing her to transcend boundaries of gender and class.

DR SIMON JORDAN

Simon Jordan is a young, Harvard-educated doctor who is tasked with writing a report on Grace Marks's mental state. His involvement in her high-profile case is partly motivated by self-interest: if he is successful in finding the truth, it will encourage investment in a pioneering and career-furthering asylum he hopes to establish. Initially, the confident Simon believes he has control over women's hearts and minds: "He has been where they could never go, seen what they could never see; he has opened up women's bodies, and peered inside" (p. 94). But while Simon takes his task seriously, he is unable to view Grace in a scientific light, and the real Grace eludes and attracts him in equal measure. Drawn into the story of Grace's life, Simon is unable to rein in his fantasies of her, ultimately losing his grip on reality and embarking on a salacious affair with his landlady. Grace refuses to be known by Simon, and for him, not knowing is "as bad as being haunted" (p. 490). Mentally unstable and physically injured by the end of the book, Simon never writes his report on Grace; instead, he becomes an entirely passive figure whose ultimate fate is to be nursed by his mother and a woman he will marry but does not love.

MARY WHITNEY

Grace looks back at the time spent working with Mary Whitney at Mrs Alderman Parkinson's house as "the happiest time of [her] life" (p. 209). Described as "fun-loving, and very mischievous and bold in her speech" (p. 173), Mary detests the class system she is oppressed by and warns Grace (who is slightly younger than her) of gentlemen who "think they are entitled to whatever they want" (p. 190). But Mary herself falls victim to one such gentleman, Mrs Alderman Parkinson's son George, and dies after having his child aborted. Grace finds her friend dead in the middle of the night and, the next day, thinks she can hear Mary's spirit talking to her. Later, after Nancy's murder, Grace "borrow[s]" (p. 169) Mary's name, using it as an alias when on the run. At one point when Mary was still alive, Mary wraps Grace up in a sheet and jokes that she looks like a madwoman; this foreshadows the hypnosis scene where, under a trance, Grace speaks in the "coarse" (p. 173) voice and sexually explicit language of Mary Whitney, leading some to believe she is possessed by her spirit.

NANCY MONTGOMERY

Nancy is Thomas Kinnear's housekeeper who lives as his wife and is pregnant with his illegitimate child when she is murdered at her home in Richmond Hill. When Grace first meets Nancy, she reminds her of her dear friend Mary, but Grace later loses respect for her, describing her as "changeable" (p. 261) and "two-faced" (*ibid.*). Nancy and Grace's relationship deteriorates, though it is unclear from Grace's narration who was more jealous of whom. Before he is hanged, James McDermott claims that it was Grace who instigated Nancy's murder, and stripped her of her clothes and gold earrings after the deed was done. But Grace insists she cannot remember what happened.

THOMAS KINNEAR

Before he is ultimately shot by James McDermott, Thomas Kinnear seems more liberal than any of Grace's previous employers, and when they first meet he allows her to sit in the front of his wagon rather than in the back "like a piece of luggage" (p. 240) However, there are signs that after Nancy he may hope to make Grace his next romantic conquest, which may have been Nancy's reason for dismissing Grace. When Dr Jordan asks Grace whether Thomas made "improper advances" (p. 373) towards her, she replies, "only what was usual" (*ibid.*), and at one point Grace catches him eyeing her bottom as she scrubs the floor on all fours. However, Thomas remains a rather enigmatic figure throughout Grace's story.

JAMES MCDERMOTT

James McDermott, Grace's alleged accomplice, is an ill-tempered, rebellious stable hand who can barely contain his contempt for Nancy Montgomery throughout her employment of him. In court, he continues to blame Grace Marks for Nancy's death right up until his public hanging, saying she convinced him to do it in return for sex. But given the effect McDermott has had on Grace's life, he occupies a relatively small part of her story.

JEREMIAH THE PEDDLER/DR JEROME DUPONT

Jeremiah is a trickster character who glides effortlessly between identities. When he first meets her, Jeremiah ambiguously tells Grace "you are one of us" (p. 179), perhaps referring to her ability to manipulate her own identity. After failing to convince Grace to escape Richmond Hill and join him on his traveling magic show, Jerome later assumes the role of the neuro-hypnotism expert Dr Jerome DuPont. DuPont seems genuinely astonished when the hypnotism he performs on

Grace takes a dark, unexpected turn, although it is worth noting that, prior to the procedure, he takes Grace aside for a conversation that neither the reader nor the other characters are privy to. As such, it is entirely possible that the whole episode is an act, though this is never made clear to the reader one way or another.

ANALYSIS

NEEDLEWORK AND NARRATIVE

Grace's natural skill in needle-work is, perhaps unexpectedly, central to her character and to the novel's main themes. Quilt-making, in particular, is integral to *Alias Grace* to such an extent that each of its chapters takes its name from different quilting patterns. However, while needlework may seem like ineffectual, innocuous women's work, chapter titles such as "Snake Fence", "Broken Dishes", or "Pandora's Box" seem dangerous and ominous, often foreshadowing narrative details within. Furthermore, Grace works on her quilts at the same time as she tells her story to Dr Jordan, thus establishing an explicit link between narrative and needlework.

The idea of creating, or refusing to create, a coherent whole from different patches of material is seen in both the way Grace tells stories and the way Simon interprets them. Grace knows that if she is to have any power (after her story itself is taken from her by a man, the lawyer, who told her what to say in court), it will come from the way she embroiders the truth. When she is deciding what to tell Dr Jordan, she muses that she could "pick out this or that for him, some bits of cloth you might say, as when you go through the rag bag looking for something that will do" (p. 43). But just as Grace chooses what to put in, she also chooses what to leave out: when Grace says that "sometimes I just bite the thread off with my teeth" (p. 71), this could refer equally to a literal thread as to the thread of a story, which she often deliberately 'cuts short'. Quilt-making is thus at the heart of discerning truth from lies; Grace says that "you can see them two different ways, by looking at the dark pieces, or else the light" (p. 187). A whole, then, can contain a multiplicity of truths.

Quilt-making is also a highly intimate act. When Simon asks Grace what quilt she would make for herself, she refuses to tell him as if it were a deeply personal secret – before confiding in the reader that it would be a 'Tree of Paradise'. She also notes that quilts are most often found on beds, the most intimate of spaces: "what we sleep in, and where we dream, and where we die" (p. 186). For women in particular, beds can be highly dangerous places – the site of death in childbirth, or else of "an indignity which they must suffer through" (*ibid.*). Where, for Grace, quilting alludes to the private, the individual, for Simon it is erotic, perhaps because of its very secrecy. For example, Simon notes at one point that "She wet the end of the thread in her mouth [...] and this gesture seemed to him all at once both completely natural and completely intimate" (p. 105). Here the mouth and the thread are one, becoming both the site of storytelling and the site of intimacy. Just as Grace sews her story, she seems to be sewing Simon deeper and deeper into it. In this way, women's needlework, often a symbol of female passivity, is quietly transformed into one of power.

MYRIAD IDENTITIES

At the end of the book, Grace does indeed make her 'Tree of Paradise' quilt. Into it, she weaves material from Mary Whitney's petticoat, her old prison attire, and a dress which once belonged to Nancy Montgomery. "And so", she says, "we will all be together" (p. 534). This could just be an expression of female solidarity, but it also seems chilling in light of the fact that Grace wore Nancy's clothes both after killing her and at the trial for her murder. The idea of several individuals being contained within a whole reminds the reader of Grace's definition of madness: "when you go mad you don't go any other place, you stay where you are. And somebody else comes in" (p. 37).

During the hypnosis, it does indeed seem that the spirit of the dead Mary Whitney is inside Grace, inhabiting her. However, Grace's identity is not as simple as a "double consciousness" (p. 471); her identities are myriad, from donning Nancy's clothes, to using Mary as an alias when on the run, to being painted as various stereotypes through history, with others appropriating and manipulating her story: she is at one and the same time murderess, innocent pawn, simpleton, beautiful sexual object, and sly manipulator. The fact that Atwood titles her book *Alias Grace* emphasises this fact: however much the reader is drawn into Grace's story, they cannot truly know her.

MATERIAL AND ETHEREAL

In dreams, of course, anything is permitted, and identities can be entirely fluid. In *Alias Grace*, Atwood foregrounds the uneasy coexistence in Victorian society of superstition and science, of the tensions between what can and cannot be proved. At one point, Simon muses:

> "What mysteries remain to be revealed in the nervous system, that web of structures both material and ethereal, that network of threads that runs throughout the body, composed of a thousand Ariadne's clues, all leading to the brain, that shadowy central den where the human bones lie scattered and the monsters lurk" (p. 217).

Here, the scientific "web of structures" becomes the stuff of myth within a single sentence, culminating in "shadows", "clues", and "monsters". This tension between reality and dream, known and unknown, can also be seen in the various reactions to what happened during Grace's hypnosis – was Grace experiencing a possession (which had been discredited for many years) or the 'doubling of consciousness' that Simon describes? Before the session, Simon had scoffed at the idea of hypnosis, but as an observer of it, the hairs stand up on the back of his neck, and he is drawn into its theatricality as he is drawn into Grace's story.

Knowability is also a question of power. In terms of their positions in society, Simon and Grace are worlds apart. While he is a male, Harvard-educated, moneyed medical professional, she is a servant, an Irish immigrant, and a woman. Occupying his initial position of power, Simon realises he desires to simultaneously control and rescue Grace: "He'll pry her out of it. He's got the hook in her mouth, but can he pull her out?" (p. 374), he says, shortly before saying he thinks of his job as "a rescue, surely he does" (*ibid.*). Simon hopes that he can extract a linear, accurate narrative from Grace, passing from a state of ignorance to knowledge – but in fact, the more Grace talks, the more lost he feels. This is a source of both intellectual and sexual frustration to him, as his attraction to Grace lies in her unknowability, as well as in her potential guilt: to him, the word 'murderess' has "an allure, a scent almost" (p. 453).

What perplexes Simon most is the fact that, while Grace can remember the minutiae of certain scenes and details from many years ago, she claims partial amnesia when it comes to the events of the murder. These gaps in memory take place while Grace is in a dream-like state, experiencing vivid hallucinations. Whether knowingly or unknowingly, Grace's story is censored (she knows this too, imagining herself at one point being pulled apart like a peach inside which there is a cold stone), and Simon begins to fill in the tantalising gaps. As his fantasies about Grace take hold of him he is drawn into a salacious affair with his landlady. But the first time he makes love to her, he believes he is dreaming, and from this point the boundaries between dreams and reality become blurred. Eventually, an inversion of power takes place: Dr Jordan appears to be the hysterical heroine, governed entirely by his own fantasies, while Grace assumes the character of a shrewd observer, at one point looking at Simon as if "she were contemplating the subject of some unexplained experiment" (p. 68). And eventually, he loses memory of the time at Kingston with amnesia that parallels Grace's. His report on Grace remains unwritten; ultimately, she does not become his 'subject' – nor, indeed, his object.

HISTORICAL TRUTH

The question of what can and cannot be known for sure is central to the genre of historical fiction. Margaret Atwood published Alias Grace in 1996, after many years of fascination with the Kinnear-Montgomery murders, whose salacious and gruesome details she read about in Susanna Moodie's (Canadian author, 1803-1885) *Life in the Clearings* (1853), which presents Grace as the instigator of Nancy's murder. But the more research she undertook, the closer to fiction Moodie's account appeared, favouring as it did the melodramatic over the meticulous. Though Atwood has stated that *"Alias Grace* is very much a novel rather than a documentary" (Atwood, 1998: 1515), she set herself strict guidelines when writing it, stating that "when there was a solid fact, I could not alter it" (*ibid*.); indeed, the book is interspersed with extracts from real historical documents.

Crucially, Atwood makes the decision to retain the ambiguity of the case rather than to solve it. Unlike some men in the story, she refuses to imprison Grace with her own discourse, knowing that Grace's power is born from her secrecy: "I have to conclude that, although there undoubtedly was a truth – someone did kill Nancy – truth is sometimes unknowable, at least by us" (*ibid*.). Within the ambiguous narrative style of *Alias Grace*, the reader is constantly made to question the truth of what they are being told; to what extent is Grace Marks simply an alias? Perhaps, as for Simon, our attraction to Grace's story lies in its very unknowability.

FURTHER REFLECTION

SOME QUESTIONS TO THINK ABOUT...

- In what ways do the characters of Simon Jordan and Grace Marks mirror each other throughout the book?
- In what ways are the characters' identities dependent on their social class? Which characters, if any, are able to transcend this class?
- Throughout the book there are many examples of biblical imagery. Where do these examples occur?
- How do you feel about the truth of Grace's guilt or innocence not being revealed? Why do you think Margaret Atwood has made this literary decision?
- Do you believe that Jeremiah's hypnosis of Grace, and the voice of Mary Whitney, was just an act? What is the evidence for and against this theory?
- Discuss the ways in which characters project their own ideas and prejudices on Grace.

- Pick out the items of clothing that play a key role in Grace's trial. What is the significance of each?

We want to hear from you!
Leave a comment on your online library
and share your favourite books on social media!

FURTHER READING

REFERENCE EDITION

- Atwood, M. (2017) *Alias Grace*. London: Virago.

REFERENCE STUDIES

- Atwood, M. (1998) In Search of Alias Grace: On Writing Canadian Historical Fiction. *The American Historical Review*. 103(5), pp. 1503-1516.
- Klemesrud, J. (1982) 'High Priestess of Angst'. *The New York Times*. [Online]. [Accessed 31 January 2019]. Available from: <http://movies2.nytimes.com/books/00/09/03/specials/atwood-angst.html>

ADDITIONAL SOURCES

- Howells, C. A. ed. (2007) *The Cambridge Companion to Margaret Atwood*. Cambridge: Cambridge University Press.

ADAPTATIONS

- *Alias Grace* (2017) [TV series]. Mary Harron. Dir. USA: Netflix

MORE FROM BRIGHTSUMMARIES.COM

- Reading guide – *The Blind Assassin* by Margaret Atwood.

- Reading guide – *The Handmaid's Tale* by Margaret Atwood.

www.brightsummaries.com

Ebook EAN: 9782808017923

Paperback EAN: 9782808017930

Legal Deposit: D/2019/12603/63

Cover: © Primento

Digital conception by Primento, the digital partner of publishers.